YOUR KNOWLEDGE HAS

- We will publish your bachelor's and
  master's thesis, essays and papers

- Your own eBook and book -
  sold worldwide in all relevant shops

- Earn money with each sale

Upload your text at www.GRIN.com
and publish for free

Bibliographic information published by the German National Library:

The German National Library lists this publication in the National Bibliography; detailed bibliographic data are available on the Internet at http://dnb.dnb.de .

Imprint:

Copyright © 2015 GRIN Verlag, Open Publishing GmbH
Print and binding: Books on Demand GmbH, Norderstedt Germany
ISBN: 9783668276369

This book at GRIN:

http://www.grin.com/en/e-book/337906/secure-data-transmission-between-an-nfc-tag-and-an-nfc-enabled-smartphone

Siddharth Sharma

Secure data transmission between an NFC tag and an NFC enabled smartphone

GRIN Publishing

GRIN - Your knowledge has value

Since its foundation in 1998, GRIN has specialized in publishing academic texts by students, college teachers and other academics as e-book and printed book. The website www.grin.com is an ideal platform for presenting term papers, final papers, scientific essays, dissertations and specialist books.

Visit us on the internet:

http://www.grin.com/

http://www.facebook.com/grincom

http://www.twitter.com/grin_com

Secure data transmission between an NFC tag and an NFC enabled smartphone.

21st August, 2015

Table of Contents

Abstract

NFC technology is considered extremely secure for communication and the number of phone that can support NFC is also at a rise. The technology is gaining worldwide recognition and as it is easy to implement and since it is really economical a numerous applications are using it. Most of NFC applications involves usage of tags, which can easily be duplicated or can be replaced by a fake one easily. Therefore, though the technology is so useful and secure, this weakness makes it vulnerable to certain attacks.

NFC has numerous application but in this thesis, I will be discussing various security threats related to NFC applications involving NFC tag and an NFC enabled smartphone For example smart posters. This thesis will evaluate various security threats like phishing, exposure to adult content etc., what they are and how an attacker can carry out these attacks. Thesis will also discuss about what an artificial neural network (ANN) is and how can it be used to eliminate these threats. The thesis also proposes a security model that will use ANN, to provide security against threats and will also provide user confidentiality, anonymity and privacy, and a category classifier to increase the overall efficiency of the model and to decrease the memory usage, and will also provide user an added feature of personalizing his security according to his requirements.

Chapter 1

Introduction

The primary goal of this thesis is to provide appropriate security checks to the data scanned, by a smartphone, from an NFC tag. As we know, the biggest advantage of using NFC instead of using any other technology for data transmission is that the data transmission rate is extremely quick, thus counter-measures should be implemented in such a manner that it should not affect the transmission rate i.e. transmission rate shouldn't be decreased.

Apart from basic security the proposed model in the thesis will provide user anonymity, confidentiality and privacy. The structure of the report is as follow

- **Chapter 2** provides a basic idea about NFC technology. In this chapter the reader will study about how the NFC works and how the data is transmitted between two NFC devices. This chapter will also discuss about cryptography, artificial neural network and category classifier.
- **Chapter 3** will discuss about the various attacks that can possess security threats to NFC technology. In this chapter I have also discussed the effect of these attacks on user's privacy and have also put some light on how an attacker can implement these attacks.
- **Chapter 4** discusses about various counter-measures that can be implemented in order to protect user from getting exposed to these attacks. It will also discuss about few useful approaches or methodologies that has been implemented in past to provide security and will examine how effectively these methodologies can train an artificial neural network (ANN).
- **Chapter 5** will reveal the **proposed security model** and will disclose the construction and working of this model. Each step of the model is discussed in detail i.e. how it works, its main components, how it not only helps in achieving the primary goal of the thesis but also provide other security feature and user added feature of personalising his security according to his requirements.
- **Chapter 6** concludes the thesis and also discuss the any future work possible.

Chapter 2

Background

In this section I will show what NFC technology is, how it operates in three different modes and its various applications. I will also discuss about NFC tags like what are the different types of NFC tags, how they communicate with NFC enabled devices and how much data they can store. As my project is about how an NFC tag embedded in a smart poster can be exploited, we will also discuss how the data after being scanned from the tag is processed by the smartphone.

2.1 Near Field Communication

(Faulkner, 2015) Suggests that NFC is a unique contactless communication technology which allows two devices placed in close proximity (distance between two devices shouldn't be more than 10 cm) to connect and transfer data quickly, without using internet. In any NFC communication there are two devices, one is known as active device, also known as reader, and the other one is known as passive device. Sometimes the communication can also take place between two active devices, example communication between two NFC enabled smartphone. According to (NearFieldCommunication.org, n.d.), the passive device usually stores the information that is read by the active devices over a radio frequency band of 13.56 MHz NFC tags embedded in a smart poster can be treated as an example of a passive tag.

NFC devices operate in three modes –

- Tag Reader/Writer
- Peer to Peer
- Card Emulation

2.1.1 Tag Reader/Writer Mode

In this mode of operation the communication takes place between an active device and a passive device. For example, reading an NFC tag embedded in a smart poster using a smart phone. Here, NFC tag is the passive device and smartphone will act as an active device. NFC tag embedded in the poster can contain any information depending upon for what purpose that poster is used. The NFC tag can contain information about any special offers that company is providing or information about a new product that the company will be launching in near future or can just have the company's URL, which will take the customer directly to the company's website. The NFC tag is a passive device because it can only store data and is not capable of reading any other NFC tag, whereas NFC enabled smart phone can read and even write data on any NFC tag thus it act as an active device or can also be called a reader (Forum, n.d.).

2.1.2 Peer to Peer Mode

In this mode of operation, the communication takes place between two active devices, or in other words between two NFC enabled devices. Example of this type of communication can be sharing contact details between two NFC enabled smart phones, or to exchange photos or any other data. This is done by just tapping or bring two NFC enabled smart phones in close proximity (Forum, n.d.). Also according to (Forum, n.d.) "Peer-to-peer mode is standardized on the ISO/IEC 18092 standard and based on NFC Forum's Logical Link Control Protocol Specification."

2.1.3 Card Emulation Mode

This mode is mainly used for financial transaction i.e. a user can use this mode to pay for purchased good or for buying ticket. The NFC enabled device used in this mode is known as or act like a smart card. Examples of NFC enabled devices acting as a smart card are credit card, smart phones etc. In this mode the communication take place between an NFC enabled device and a remote card reader. The biggest advantage of using this mode is that even if a normal credit card is converted into an NFC enable device i.e. into a smart card, by embedding an NFC chip in the card, it will still work as normal. And by just embedding an NFC chip in the card reader, used to read the conventional contactless cards, we can use it to read our smart card, thus not forcing us to change the existing infrastructure (Forum, n.d.).

2.2 NFC tags

NFC tags comes under the category of passive tags i.e. they are not capable of reading or writing data on any other tag. They can be used for various purposes like they can be embedded in a smart poster or can be embedded on a wristband or can be embedded in a visiting card or in any application where we don't need to transfer or store big data. They can be read or written by an active NFC enabled devices like smartphones. URLs are the most preferred form of data to be stored on an NFC tag as they take very less space and can contain a lot of information. For example, by storing a URL on an NFC tag embedded into a smart poster, a company can redirect the customers to their website, where they have displayed latest offers rather than storing all the offers on the tag itself (Poole, n.d.).

Taking in the consideration the format and the capacity of a tag, NFC tags are divided into 4 different types. According to (Poole, n.d.) "These NFC tag type formats are based on ISO 14443 Types A and B which is the international standard for contact-less smartcards) and Sony FeliCa which conforms to ISO 18092, the passive communication mode, standard)."

2.2.1 Tag types
Different types of NFC tags are –

- **Tag Type 1** – Based on ISO14443A type 1 tags are the most cost effective tags. Since, only 96 bytes of memory is available, upgradable up to 2kbyte, to store data they are suitable for applications which doesn't need a lot of memory space like storing URL of a website. These tags can be re written and they communicate at a speed of 106 Kbit/s. Though they are capable of re-writing data but a user, if he wants, can deprive the tag with this capability and can make it a read-only tag. For example, a company can use this property of type 1 tag in their smart poster. After writing the company's URL on the tag they can configure the tag in such a manner that it can't be re-written. Now anyone can read the tag but no one can write anything on the tag, thus protecting the data from getting modified (Poole, n.d.).

- **Tag Type 2** – Type 2 is almost similar to type 1 i.e. they are based on ISO14443A standard and are rewritable (Poole, n.d.). As in type 1, type 2 tag also provide user with an option of making the tag read-only. Type 2 tag provide data collision protection and communicate at a speed similar to that of type 1 i.e. 106 Kbit/s. The only difference between type 1 and type 2 is that type 1 have 96 bytes of memory to store data whereas type 2 just have 48 bytes of memory which can be upgraded to 2 Kbyte. Type 2 tags can also be used for storing URLs but user tends to prefer type 1 tag over type 2 as the later provides less default memory space (NearFieldCommunication.org, n.d.).
- **Tag Type 3** – Sometimes called as FeliCa, type 3 are compatible with JIS X 6319-4. Unlike type 1 and type 2, once a type 3 is configured as read and re-writable or as read-only a user cannot re-configure it. They communicate at a speed of 212 Kbit/s or 424 Kbit/s and have variable memory limit up to 1 Mbyte (Cassidy, 2007).
- **Tag Type 4** – Based on ISO14443A and B standards they communicate at a speed up to 424 Kbit/s. They can store data up to 32 Kbytes and are either, read and re-writable or read only (Cassidy, 2007).

2.3 NFC Data Exchange Format (NDEF)

To exchange data structures through NFC, few formats and rules needs to defined and this is done by NFC data exchange format i.e. NDEF (Roland & Langer, 2010). A message called NDEF message containing the NDEF record and the data is transmitted through NFC (Developers, n.d.). NDEF records contain application specific data structures and type information (Roland & Langer, 2010).

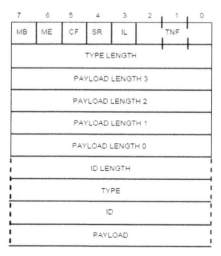

Fig.1 NDEF RECORD

7

As shown in Fig.1 in an NDEF record there is a payload field and multiple header fields. (Roland & Langer, 2010) Insists that the header has following flags –

- Message Begin (MB) – It is the first record of an NDEF message.
- Message End (ME) – It is the last record of an NDEF message.
- Chunk Flag (CF) – It can be set to two values 1 or 0, where 1 means the current record contains the payload partially and the rest of the payload is in the next record.
- Short Record (SR) – It can also be set to 1 or 0 and indicates the size of the payload length (PL) field, where 1 means the PL is a 1-byte unsigned integer and 1 refers to 4-byte unsigned integer.
- ID Length Present (IL) – It can also be set to 1 or 0, where 1 means the field is present whereas 0 states its absence. Any unique identifier can be specified using this field.

According to (Roland & Langer, 2010) , "The value of the TNF field determines the format of the type information:
- 0h: The record is empty. The fields Type, ID and Payload are not present and their length fields are set to zero.
- 1h: The Type field contains the relative URI (Uniform Resource Identifier) of an NFC Forum well-known type according to the NFC Record Type Definition (RTD).
- 2h: The Type field contains a MIME media type identifier (RFC 2046).
- 3h: The Type field contains an absolute URI (RFC 3986).
- 4h: The Type field contains the relative URI of an NFC Forum external type according to the RTD.
- 5h: The record contains data in an unknown format. No type information is present and the length of the Type field is zero.
- 6h: The record continues the payload of the preceding chunked record. No type information is present and the length of the Type field is zero.
- 7h: Reserved for future use."

The main data that is stored in the payload is processed according to the above mentioned values.

2.4 Reading NDEF data from an NFC tag

According to (Developers, n.d.)," Reading NDEF data from an NFC tag is handled with the tag dispatch system, which analyses discovered NFC tags, appropriately categorizes the data, and starts an application that is interested in the categorized data. An application that wants to handle the scanned NFC tag can declare an intent filter and request to handle the data." It means when NDEF data, which is stored on the tag, is scanned by an NFC enabled device, the device tries to find the most appropriate application to handle the scanned data. This is done in order to make sure that a user is not asked to manually choose an application, as it might cause the connection between the tag and the device to break (Developers, n.d.). Tag dispatch system handles the NDEF data, finds an appropriate application to handle that data and on finding one passes the data to the application. For examples if the tag contains a URL, the tag dispatch system passes it to the web browser. The browser, without asking the user, runs the URL in the browser (Developers, n.d.).

One thing that attracts attention here is that the scanned data is handed to an appropriate application based on the type of the data i.e. if it's a URL it is sent to a browser or if it's an image it is opened in the gallery. The data dispatch system does not actually check whether the data has been modified in an unauthorised manner or in case of URL it doesn't check whether the link is redirecting a user to a legitimate page or to a phishing page. In the later chapter's we will see what security threats this property can cause and how badly it can effect a user.

2.5 Cryptography

Cryptography is a technique which allows individuals to share secret or important information in a more secure or secret way. For example, imagine two people, say Alice and Bob, who shared important secret have to split up. This require them to share private information from a distance. However an eavesdropper, also wants this information, and has the ability to intercept their messages. So, now Alice can communicate with Bob by locking her message in a box, using a lock that is only known to her and Bob. This locking of the message can be called as **encryption.** And then sending the message over to Bob. On receiving the box, Bob opens up the lock using the key they shared in advance and reads the message. This unlocking of message is known as **decryption. Cryptography** begins when we replace physical locks with **ciphers.** The cipher allows both Alice and Bob to scramble and descramble their messages so that they would appear meaningless to an eavesdropper, who tries to intercept their message.

(Kessler, 2015) Says that cryptography can provide –

- **Authentication** – Proving one's identity to other.
- **Privacy/confidentiality** – Ensuring that no eavesdropper can read the message.
- **Integrity** – It means that the receiver received the exact same message that was sent by the sender i.e. it wasn't modified. Cryptography can't prevent modification but can **identify** any modification.
- **Non-repudiation** – It means the message was actually sent by the sender and not by an imposter.

2.5.1 Symmetric Key Cryptography

Symmetric key cryptography, also known as secret key cryptography, means performing encryption and decryption using the same key. In this type of cryptography the sender and the receiver knows each other, in any way, in advance and shares a secret. This secret key is first, used to encrypt a plain text into a cipher text. The cipher text is transmitted to the receiver, who uses the same key to decrypt the cipher text and obtains the plain text (Ayushi, 2010).

Advantages of using symmetric key cryptography are –

- It is faster as compared to public key system.
- Easy to implement and doesn't require high processing power.
- Identity authentication is achievable.

Disadvantages of using symmetric key cryptography are –

- Key distribution is really difficult
- Brute force attack can be used to crack it (Clercq, 2006).

2.5.2 Public Key Cryptography

In public key cryptography, instead of using the same key for encryption and decryption, there are two keys one for encryption and one for decryption. It is also known as asymmetric key cryptography. In this cryptography system, both sender and receiver have two keys. One of the key is known as **public key**, it is known to everyone one, and the other key is known as **private key**, it is only known to themselves. The sender encrypts the plaintext using receiver's public key and sends it to the receiver. Receiver on receiving the cipher text uses his private key to decrypt it and obtain the plain text. The receiver now, encrypts the reply with sender's public key and sends it over. The sender decrypts it using his private key and obtains the plain text (Ayushi, 2010). Even if the attacker knows the cipher text and the public key of the sender or the receiver, it is still almost impossible to obtain the private key of the sender or the receiver.

Advantage of public key cryptography are-

- Key distribution is easy.
- They are securer than symmetric key cryptography as data can only be decrypted if the attacker has the public key, which is almost impossible to obtain.

Disadvantages of public key cryptography –

- Slower as compared to symmetric key cryptography.
- Requires high computational power and are more complex (Dunning, n.d.).

2.6 Artificial Neural Network (ANN)

The problems we face in digital world are often complex and it takes considerable amount of time and hardware to solve these problems. One competent way to solve and understand such complex problems can be by breaking them into simpler elements (Gershenson, n.d.) And logically connecting them to each other. This logical connections can also be known as a network.

One type of such network is artificial neural network. (Gurney, 2004) Insists that "A neural network is an interconnected assembly of simple processing elements, units or nodes, whose functionality is loosely based on the animal neuron. The processing ability of the network is stored in the inter unit connection strengths, or weights, obtained by a process of adaptation to, or learning from, a set of training patterns."

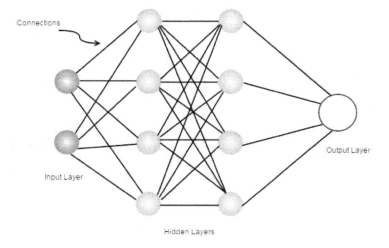

Fig.2 Basic Neural Network

When an input is given, it is exchanged between different neuron through these interconnections. Each connection has some mathematical weight and based on the experience these weights are adjusted accordingly. Thus allowing the network to adjust according the input and making it capable of learning. "This process of adjusting the weights is called learning or training" (Gershenson, n.d.) .

There are two ways in which they can be trained, namely-

- **Unsupervised Training** or Self-Organising ANN – In this type of training data is collected in abundance and is given as an input to the ANN. ANN tries to "discover patterns and relationships in that data" (Kay, 2001). This type of training is advantageous when we wants to analyse data outputted by an experiment (Kay, 2001).
- **Supervised Training** – As the name suggest this type of training is supervised by a trainee or a teacher. Teacher serves the network with certain input values, whose output values are known to him. The network processes the input and outputs a value and that value is cross checked with expected output. On receiving the correct output, the teacher re-uses the neural weights that were responsible in producing that output. On the other hand, on receiving a negative or incorrect output, the weights are discarded (Kay, 2001). This type of training helps to minimise the chances of outputting a wrong or incorrect value.

Once the training is completed, an ANN can be used for problem-solving applications, security purposes detecting anomalies or any specific pattern of data, character recognition etc. ANN can be implemented on a single computer but the processing will be slower as compared to other algorithmic solutions. But this problem can be resolved, if the ANN is implemented on a parallel platform i.e. rather than using a single processor, multiple processors are used in its construction.

This not only makes the processing faster but also improves the data processing efficiency of the network (Kay, 2001).

In the later chapters we will see how ANN can be used in a near field communication environment and how effectively can it solve major NFC security threats.

2.7 Category Classifier

Category classifier means classifying the scanned URL from the tag into a specific category like adult, sports, social networking etc. This category classification will play an important role in the **proposed security model** (discussed in chapter 5).

A scanned URL can be classified in two ways –

- It can be classified manually or by examining HTML structure of the web page
- Or it can be classified using the already existing site classifiers like Zvelo, WebPulse Site Review Request, URL/IP Lookup, Cyren etc.

According to (Attardi, et al., n.d.) "examination of structure of a HTML document starts from a list of URLs, retrieving the documents referred by each of them and analysing the structure of the document expressed in terms of its HTML tags.

Any URL found during the analysis is passed back to the spidering process if it points to a document within the current site, and stored for later analysis if it points to an external site. This allows to perform a depth-first visit of a site, collecting any categorization information it contains about itself and other sites. The categorization task exploits the database of URL *context paths* and the *category tree* within which the URL must be categorized. The category tree consists of a tree, where each node contains a *title*, i.e. a single word or phrase, which identifies the category. The goal of the categorization is to find the most appropriate categories to which a URL should belong."

Or, when a URL is scanned it can be sent to the already existing sites, which classifies web pages using their pre-determined classifying algorithms. So now, when user's smartphone scans a tag, the URL stored on that tag is processed by the smartphone and is sent to the **category classifier.** The category classifier can have the links to the above mentioned URL classifier sites, so when the user sends a link to the classifier, it is classified on the basis of the category output by these sites. Or the classifier can directly analyse the HTML structure and can accordingly output a category.

Chapter 3

NFC Security Threats

As we studied in section 2.4, when an NFC enabled phone scans an NFC tag it opens the content stored on the NFC tag using the most suitable application. The selection of the most suitable application depends upon the type of data (pdf, URL etc.) stored on the NFC tag and is independent of the data that is stored on it. This property or flaw assists hackers in carrying out attacks like --

- Exposure to adult/objectionable content
- Phishing
- Automated malware download from malicious web pages

Apart from these three attacks there are various other security threats, such as-

- Eavesdropping
- Data corruption
- Data modification
- Cloning

3.1 Exposure to Adult/Objectionable content

Paedophiles, hate literature, violence, pornography are few typical examples of adult or objectionable content. The sort of data these contents contain and the negative effect that they can have on the web users has made it one of the biggest social issues that needs to be resolve (Choi, et al., August 2005). An attacker can expose teenage and other web users to such content by just re-writing or replacing a legitimate NFC tag with one containing adult content. For example, an organisation ABC is launching a new product and for its promotion they make use of smart posters. They embed every poster with an NFC tag, the NFC tag contains the company's URL which when scanned by the user, directs the user to the company's website. Now, an attacker, with intent of destroying company's reputation, replaces the NFC tag embedded in to the poster with one of his tags. Say, hat replaced tag contains URL of a porn site. So, now whenever a user will scan that tag he/she will be directed to that porn site instead of the company's website. Since the NFC enabled device performed its action solely based on the type of data stored on the tag and it didn't perform any actions to check the authenticity or the credibility of the data, the attacker was successful in launching this attack.

3.2 Phishing

(Ding & Pan, 2006) Insists phishing technically means luring users to a fake or deceptive website in order to steal user credentials and sometimes their identities. There are different ways in which these attacks can be performed like through phished email, social engineering or by creating a fake page of a legitimate web page. Also according to (Poly, et al., 2012), "the problem can be defined as the inability of the architecture to detect that the identity and the content of an information item do not match, i.e., the architecture cannot realize that a phishing page contains information regarding an item X but its name is Y."

An attacker can even carry out this attack by manipulating an NFC tag. For example, an attacker can either replace the NFC tag embedded on a smart poster by his, which contains URL of a bogus website. Thus can redirect a user directly to that fake page and can steal his credentials. And often NFC tags are used to setup Wi-Fi connection. If an attacker manipulates the content of that tag then "the visitor could get the wrong connection information and will connect to a malicious access point (AP) believing they were connected to the right one. All traffic such as surfing the web which does not use higher level end-to-end security (i.e. SSL/TLS) could then be intercepted by the attacker" (Kilas, 2009).

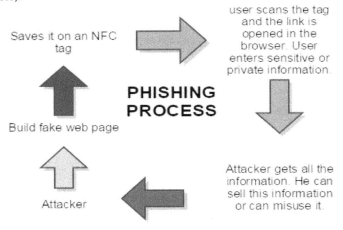

Fig.3 Phishing Process

An attacker can also perform this attack by changing the content of an NFC tag. The attacker can put his phished page URL on the tag or can change the already written URL on the tag in such a manner that it will redirect the user to the attacker's phished page. A user will never be able to identify this change as, when a URL is scanned by the smartphone, from an NFC tag, the smartphone doesn't check whether the URL is redirecting the user to the webpage as indicated in the URL or to any other webpage. It just processes the scanned data and on finding out that it is a URL, directly opens it in the browser.

Sometimes, the URL is displayed on the user's screen before being opened in the browser. But the user can't see the entire the URL and if an attacker does any modification at the end of the URL, then it can't be identified by the user. Since, this attack is easy to implement and difficult to identify, thus makes it one of the most threatening attacks.

3.3 Automated malware download and malicious web pages

An attacker can infect or compromise user's computer in various ways. He can use a malicious code to infect a machine or can upload a virus or Trojan horse on a legitimate web page, which if downloaded can have a total control over the user's machine. According to (Zhang, et al., 2009), "malicious code is a script with malicious intent that has the potential to harm the machine on which it executes. And it can even become an approach of Trojan transmission".

In NFC, an attacker can modify the data on the tag. He can over write the data present on the tag with his URL. When a user scans the tag, he will be redirected to that malicious web page and his machine will be exploited. The malicious web page can either automatically download a virus on the machine or might contain a script which might any pre-existing browser vulnerabilities. This will allow the attacker to gain access to the cookies and sensitive data, like passwords, stored in the browser.

An attacker can even make use of a legitimate looking site to infect the user's computer. For example, he can create a phished **Facebook** page and will then ask a user to sign in. When the user enter his sign in details, the details will be sent to the attacker. Similarly, he can make a phished Gmail page or even a phished bank website to compromise user's financial details. Another thing an attacker can do is, they can upload a worm on a legitimate site or can send it through email. The worm can be hidden in a pdf file or in an application or in a game. When the user opens that web page containing the worm, the worm automatically gets downloaded to the user's computer. When the user opens that pdf or runs the game, worm runs in the background, and infects the whole machine.

3.4 Eavesdropping

According to (Kilas, 2009), "because the communication is not encrypted at the link level a listening attacker might be able to read the content of the communication if no encryption is applied at higher levels." It means, in NFC, data is always transmitted in plain text and if an eavesdropper can intercept the message then he/she can easily read the message. Thus, this technology is not that safe to share sensitive data.
Having said that, NFC is still one of the safest way of communication as the communicating devices has to be very close to each other, typically less than 10 cm. An attacker, who wish to intercept the messages, has to be in the range of 1 to 10 m of the communicating devices. Thus, making it really difficult for an eavesdropper to intercept the message. But use of appropriate equipment can allow an eavesdropper to read the content of the message and even hinder user's privacy. Privacy hindrance can be explained with this example, NFC tags usually have unique IDs, to differentiate one tag from other. An attacker can place a hidden reader, say at the entrance of an underground station. So now, whenever a user will pass by that reader, the reader will read and store the unique ID of the tag. This ID can bot even reveal personal details of a user but will also tell an attacker that at what time was user present at that underground station i.e. this ID can also be used to track an individual. Thus hindering their privacy (Kilas, 2009).

3.5 Data Corruption

(Rajaram, et al., 2014) Said that "this attack is also known as 'Denial of Service' attack in which an attacker interferes with data transmission, disturbing or blocking data such that the receiver is not able to decipher the data. The attacker transmits radio signals to reduce the signals to random noises destroying the information content". The attacker's main motive behind this type of attack is not to read or intercept the message that is being transfer. His main aim is to deny the receiver from accessing certain services or to just corrupt the data in such a manner that on entering an input value the user will not get the desired output (Sharma, et al., 2013). Thus, corrupting and disturbing the entire communication.

3.6 Data Modification

This attack is many times mistaken as data corruption attack, but it is very different from the data corruption attack. In this attack, the attacker doesn't want to disturb the communication or doesn't want to deny receiver from certain services, rather he wants to receive a valid data and then modify the data sent by the sender before it reaches the receiver (Abd Allah, 2011). He can delete the transmitted data so that the receiver never receives any data or can change the sent data by his own malicious data so that he can perform any malicious activity. An attacker can use this technique to carry out phishing attack. For example, an attacker can change the content of a tag embedded in a smart poster with his malicious URL and can redirect the user to his phished page where user's personal or financial information can be captured by the attacker. Or he can change the content of Wi-Fi setup tag, which will force user to get connected to the attacker's malicious network and all his activities can now be monitored by the attacker.

Chapter 4

Counter-Measures

We have seen in the previous chapter that how harmful and infectious NFC security threats can be. Therefore, it is important to lay down appropriate and effective counter-measures, which can make NFC a much safer way of communication. Though identifying counter-measures is an important step, their careful and systematic implementation is even more important.

Thus in this chapter, out of the above discussed threats, I will discuss about various counter measures that can be implemented to neutralise or eradicate the first three threats i.e.

- Exposure to adult/objectionable content
- Phishing
- Automated malware downloads and malicious websites

4.1 Exposure to Adult/Objectionable content

In the past few year, there is a significant rise in the number of users, especially children, which are being exposed to adult content, like porn, unwillingly while surfing internet. Sometimes they are exposed to such content through emails and sometimes through phished pages. And now, attackers have found a new way of carrying out this attack that is by manipulating data stored in an NFC tag. For example, they can change the tag that is embedded in smart poster with a tag that contains a URL of a porn site. Since, we can't stop an attacker from manipulating the tag, we must properly check the URL before opening it in the browser. This checking of adult/ objectionable content can be done in various ways.

ANN will play a significant role in fighting against this threat. ANN can be trained by initially feeding it with number of pornographic web pages or web pages containing illegal matter. It will process the pages and will look for different details like –

- Number of images per page
- How many words are highlighted on that page
- How many links does that page has to images and videos

According to the research done by (Watters & Ho, 2005), out of the total number of porno-graphic pages they evaluated, 74% of them had in excess of 5 images whereas only 32% of the total non-pornographic pages had 5 images or more. Their research also showed that 75% of the pornographic pages had more than 10% highlighted words (out of the total words on that page) and 36% of them had 11- 20 links that took the user to images or videos. On the other hand, only 0.2% of non-pornographic pages had links to videos or images and only 54% of them had 10% of their words highlighted (Watters & Ho, 2005).

Thus in the training phase, an ANN will be fed with the URL's of numerous pornographic pages and will look for the above mentioned details. It will scan the page and will output a value for different parameters i.e. it will go through the structure of the page and will look for number of images, links to different pages etc. and then will output a number. This process will take place for every single URL and once the training is completed a **threshold value** will be selected for each parameter. Now, when a URL will be processed by an ANN, it will output a value for each parameter. If that value will be less than the threshold value than that URL will be treated as non-infectious and will be added to the WL. Whereas, if the value is above the threshold value the URL will be treated as infectious and will be stored in the BL$_A$. For example, a URL www.thesis.com is fed as an input to the ANN, it will process the URL and will output values for the set parameters, say it outputs 6 for number of images present on that page and the threshold value for this parameter was 8. Then this URL will be treated as non-infectious and will be stored in the WL.

Rather than selecting an exact value for threshold we can even select a range. So, if the output value for the URL is less than that range then it will be white listed and if it is greater than that range than it will be blacklisted. Whereas, if the value for one parameter falls in the range, and values for the rest of the parameters falls below and above then if the number of parameters having value above the range is greater than the number of parameters having value less than the rage, the URL will be **black listed** .If the number of parameters having value lower than the range is greater, then the URL will be **white listed**.

Other than the above mentioned three parameters we can include some other parameters too like –

- **Detecting skin colour**, (Stahl & Ulges, 2011) "matched the detected skin regions with human bodies by applying geometric grouping rules". This can be done by feeding the ANN with thousands of objectionable images and obtaining certain vectors that can differentiate an objectionable image from a normal image (Firschein, et al., 1997). This parameter can solve two problems. Firstly, if the value of the number of image present on the page parameter is in the threshold range then this technique can be used to analysis images, and the URL can be listed accordingly. Secondly, if a user creates his own page and uploads only one or two objectionable images. Then, his URL will not be detected by the any of the above mentioned parameter but will be caught by this parameter.
- Searching harmful keywords likes sex, BDSM, terrorism, ass, bitch, cunt, fuck etc. ANN can be trained to detect these words on a web page. Though this technique can give false-positive results but if ANN is properly trained, this technique can prove useful.

All these parameter can be used together during training phase of an ANN and a database of WL & BL can be created. Now, whenever a URL will be scanned by a smartphone from an NFC tag, it will be cross-checked through this database and will be listed accordingly. If it is not matched to any value present in the database then it will be sent to the ANN which will analyse it in the similar manner as it analysed other URL during training and will output values of different parameters. These values will decided whether to discard the URL or not.

4.2 Phishing

Phishing is one of the easiest way of stealing someone's credentials. A user, by just looking at a web page, cannot judge whether it is an original page or a phished page, thus making this threat more dangerous. Though on investigating and analysing a web page in a systematic way can reveal whether the page is phished or not.

Abnormality in the URL is one way of detecting a phished page i.e. sometimes the hostname in the URL is different from the name viewed on the site (Ding & Pan, 2006). For example, an attacker can create a fake **Facebook** page under the URL www.faceboook.com. At first sight the URL might look perfectly fine, but if looked carefully the user will see that the "faceboook" in the URL contains three O's whereas the one on the web page has two. But no one now days see URL's that carefully which gives an attacker a small window of opportunity to carry out his attack.

Another way of identifying a phished page is by analysing any abnormality in the URL request or in DNS record. According to (Ding & Pan, 2006), "A phishing page usually has a high percentage of object references to its target (the real site) in order to show similar appearance. By contrast, a legitimate web page usually requests its objects from its own domain" and also many a times hostname in the URL of a phished page is not present in WHOIS database.

These two ways can be used to train an ANN i.e. an ANN will be fed with phished page and legitimate web page. It will then analyse the page and will observe where the objects are being referred in a phished page and where they are referred in a legitimate page. Thus, learning to differentiate between original and phished page based on referencing. It will also analyse the hostname and the text on the web page of both original and phished page in order to learn pattern of abnormalities that can occur. During the training, the ANN will place the phished page in the black list and the original pages in the white list. Since the trainee will already have the list of the expected outputs, he can identify any mistake executed by the ANN and can rectify it then and there .It will also discard the weights that where responsible for that output.

Alongside these two ways, an approach proposed by (Medvet, et al., 2008) can also be used to train an ANN. (Medvet, et al., 2008) proposed that a phished page can be identified by analysing and comparing the visual appearances of the phished page and the target page (legitimate page whose phished page is created). They said that if the two pages has too much similarity and not exactly similar then the user is alerted that it is a phished page. (Medvet, et al., 2008) Considered "text pieces, images embedded in the page, and the overall visual appearance of the web page as rendered by the browser to check visual similarity".
These three ways will train the ANN and will create a WL & BL_P that will be stored in the WL & BL database. Any URL scanned will be cross checked through the database and if it is not present in the database it will be analysed by the ANN and the output will be stored in the database.

4.3 Automated malware downloads and malicious websites

One way of detecting a malicious site can be by training the ANN using signature technique. In this technique signatures of viruses or malwares stored in trusted Intrusion Detection System or anti-virus applications are used to detect a malware or malicious site (Le, et al., 2011). The suspected website is analysed and matched with the stored signatures. If the signature matches then it the site is treated as malicious and if it doesn't then the site will not cause any harm to user. This technique is not that useful as it can miss the viruses or malwares, whose signatures are not stored in these IDS (Le, et al., 2011).

A much better and reliable approach to detect malicious websites is the "two-stage classification model" proposed by (Le, et al., 2011). The first stage is the extraction of the static feature, the URL is sent to the extractor which extracts the static features to analyse the maliciousness of the page. A static feature is a feature which is obtained without executing the URL. This maliciousness helps in creating two categories: harmful URL and harmless URL (Le, et al., 2011). Once the categorising is done, only the harmful URL's are sent to the second stage i.e. to Run-time feature monitor. It monitors and records the features while the URL is loaded. These features are then analysed and the URL is again categorised as harmful or harmless. If it is categorised harmful in the second stage too, then the URL is malicious and can cause damage to the user's machine, thus is discarded (Le, et al., 2011).

In this thesis I will be using this technique to train the ANN and create a WL & BL_M that will be stored in the WL & BL database.

Chapter 5

Proposed Security Model

Based on the counter measures discussed in the previous chapter I would like to propose a security model that will not only provide security against these three threats but will also provide an added feature of personal security list, privacy or secrecy and anonymity to the users.

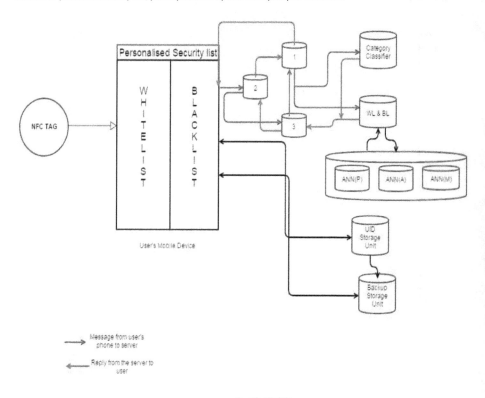

Security Model

Fig.4 Proposed Security Model

5.1 Components

NFC Tag

Tag containing information that user will be scanning.

Personal Security

It is an added feature that will allow users to personalise their security preferences. User can use this feature to create their own personal White list & Black list and these lists will be stored on their devices.

Category Classifier

It will classify incoming URLs into different categories like sports, electronics, science etc. and will work as discussed in section 2.8. It can be stored on the server side or can even be stored on the user's smartphone.

Artificial Neural Network (ANN)

Once the artificial neural network will be trained its output value will be used to produce a database of White List & Black List. Depending upon the threat to be addressed ANN can be of three different types -

- ANN(P) – ANN white listing and black listing against Phishing
- ANN(A) – ANN white listing and black listing against exposure to adult/objectionable content
- ANN(M) – ANN white listing and black listing against automated malware download and malicious websites

White List & Black List

The output from the ANN will be stored either in the black list or in the white list. The URL stored in the NFC tag, after getting scanned by the user, will be cross checked with these lists to check whether its secure for the user to open this link or not.

ID Storage Unit

It will store the UIDs (Unique Identities) that will be created when the user will sign up for the first time. These UIDs will be used throughout the communication between the application installed on the mobile device and the servers.

Back Up Storage Unit

The data stored in the user application will be automatically uploaded in this storage unit. Thus, if a user changes his mobile device, for any reason, he can back up all his data from the back up storage unit.

5.2 User Sign-Up

To use this model, user will install an application on his/her mobile phone. After installing the application, user will be asked to sign up using a valid email id and password. The email id and the password entered by the user will be sent to the UID Storage unit. The UID storage unit will be equipped with a UID generator. The UID generator will be fed with two inputs i.e. email ID and password and depending upon the input it will output a unique value. The UID generator will have three main properties

- **_Property 1_** – Whenever the same email id and password will be given as an input, the output value will be the same.
- **_Property 2_** – If any one of the two input values is changed, it will output a different value.
- **_Property 3_** – UID generator will work on the principal of One-Way function i.e. the function should be easy to compute and hard to reverse (Martin, 2012), and once the UID is created it will automatically delete user's email id and password.

So following these properties, the UID (Unique Identity) generator will take user's email id and password and will output a value. This output value will act as a Unique ID for that particular user and will be used for any communication that takes place between the application installed on the mobile device and the server.

This UID will be stored in the ID storage unit. As we know, there can be a possibility where two different users can have the same password but there is no way that they can have the same email id. Thus, for any two different users the email id input field will always be different. Therefore, UID generator output will never be same i.e. for every sign up it will output a unique value.

The UID storage unit will then send the unique ID (UID) to the user and will also create an entry against the given UID in the Back up Storage unit. Alongside the UID it will also send user and Backup Storage Unit a secret key. This key will act as a long term shared key and will be used by the user only at the time off backing up his data on to the server or retrieving it back from the server.

After successfully signing up, user will be asked a security question, like the town he/she was born or his/her favourite football team etc., the answer of this security question will be stored on the user's app and will not be sent to the ID database Unit. Now the user can use the installed application not only for -

- Basic security against malicious websites, phishing pages and preventing users from getting exposed to adult/objectionable content.

But also for providing user

- Personalised security
- Confidentiality and Data integrity
- Anonymity

5.3 Working

Whenever a user wishes to scan a tag, he will open the installed app on his phone and will bring his phone in the communicating distance of the tag and will perform following steps-

Step 1

The app will then scan the tag and will process the data, which in this case is URL, and will then send the scanned URL concatenated with the user's UID to two different parts of the server, one part will be containing WL & BL database and the other will be equipped with category classifier (if the category classifier is stored on the server), through different and random hops. This concatenated UID will act as a MAC address and the server, after processing the URL, will send back the result to this address.

Note: All this communication between the server and the application on the user side will take place over an encrypted channel. The channel can be encrypted in various ways depending upon factors like cost of implementation, level of security etc. One way of encrypting the cannel could be by using SSL encryption. According to (Martin, 2012), "SSL is a general communication security protocol for protecting data while it is being transferred between different locations. Although it has many applications, most users encounter SSL when securing a web connection between a client machine and a web server, for example, when making a purchase from an online store."

Step 2

The WL & BL database will match the URL with the values stored in the WL & BL. If any of the lists finds a value equivalent to the given URL, it will send the result to the user through different hops. Whereas, if both the lists doesn't have an equivalent value, the URL will be sent to ANN where it will be processed by the three different ANN's .Once the processing is done ANN will output a value that will be first saved in the black list or the white list on the server side and then will be sent to the user through different hops. Similarly, category classifier will classify the URL in a specific category and will send that category to the user through different hops.

Step 3

The user will receive two results. One will be the category to which that URL belongs like sports, fashion, science etc. And second result will tell whether that URL is safe to open or can possess some threat to the user. If the second result says that the URL is safe to open then the URL will be opened in the browser and when the user will close the browser a question will be pop up on the screen asking "Was this a relevant link? Or would you like to view this kind of link in future or not?" Whereas if the result says that the URL poses a threat then the application will pop up a message saying "Threat Detected" and the app will not open that link.

These three steps will provide security against phishing attack, malicious websites or automated download and exposure to adult/objectionable content. Thus, achieving the main objective of this thesis i.e. implementing appropriate security checks on the scanned data before handing it to the application, in our case it will be the web browser, that is interested in running that data.

5.3.1 Personalised Security List

Apart from this basic security, this model also provides user an added feature of creating his own personal white list & black list database i.e. **Personalised Security List(PSL)**. But before creating personalised security list we will look at the different approaches that we can opt in order to make this model more efficient. We can adapt two approaches, either we can save the URL under the category returned by the category classifier and can then black list or white list the URL depending upon the second result and the answer given by the user to that pop up question or we can directly black list or white the category returned by the category classifier and save it under user's personal security list, depending upon the second result and the user's answer to that question, and can discard the URL.

The advantage of White listing or Black listing the category and discarding the URL is that once a category is black listed or white listed we just have to categorise a given URL and if the category in which it falls is white listed then it will be white listed or if the category is black listed then the URL will be black listed. It means we don't need to keep record of hundreds of URL and cross checking a URL with a white listed or a black listed category will always be quicker than cross checking through white listed or black listed saved URLs, as list of URL will always outnumber the list of categories, thus improving the model's efficiency and also saving considerable memory space. Therefore, in this model we will be opting for the approach of white listing & black listing categories on the user side.

Now that we have selected one approach, the next challenge is to select one of the 4 possible values the other result will provide. Result coming out from the WL & BL database on the server side has 4 different values because that database is created by three different ANNs which are ANN (P) ANN (A) ANN (M).The white list created by each of them will be merged into one list designated as "WL". The black lists created by them will come under one black list designated as "BL" in the database but the outputs of that BL will be designated either as BL (A) or BL (P) or BL (M), just to let user know which ANN black listed the given URL. Thus, leaving us with four possible values –

- WL – White list created by all the three ANNs
- BL(A) – Black list created by ANN(A)
- BL(P) – Black list created by ANN(P)
- BL(M) – Black list created by ANN(M)

Using these four values, category in the result 1 and user's answer to the popped up question, the application will create user's personalised security list.

If result 2 outputs WL, then the application will process the URL and will open up the link in the browser and in the end will pop up a question saying "Was this a relevant link? Or Would you like to view this kind of link in future or not?".

1. **_White list_**- user says "YES" then the category in the result one will be "white listed".
2. **_Black list_**- But if user says "NO" then the category in the result one will be "black listed".

If result 2 outputs BL (A), then the application will black list the category present in the result one. That URL will not be opened instead a pop message will pop saying "Threat Detected". In this case the pop up question is irrelevant as the URL is already being inspected as a threat.

If result 2 outputs BL(P), then the application will **NOT** black list the **category** present in the result one but that URL will still not be opened instead a message will pop saying "Threat Detected". The category is not black listed because an attacker can create a phishing page of a website that falls in a particular category but that doesn't mean that every single web site falling in that category is phished.

If result 2 outputs BL(M), then the application will **NOT** black list the **category** present in the result one but that URL will still not be opened instead a pop message will pop saying "Threat Detected". The category is not black listed because an attacker can infect a website that falls in a particular category but that doesn't mean that every single web site falling in that category is infected.

So, in user's personalised security, a category will only be black listed if it has been black listed by ANN(A) or the user has answered "NO" to that popping question. This list is called user's personalised security list because the popping question allows the user to customize black list & white list of categories according to his interests and preferences and as every individual have different preference and interest they can use this feature to customize their own personal security list and can block any category that they don't wish to view even if that URL or category is safe to view.

Once the Personal security list starts building up, the application will work as normal, will scan the tag and send the data to the server, the server will process it and will send the result alongside the category that it falls in. Now, on receiving this result and category from the server, if the result says that the URL is black listed then depending upon the ANN, who blacklisted it, it will act as discussed above but if the result says that the URL is white listed than it will cross check the category received from the user with the categories stored in the personal security list rather than directly opening the link in the browser. If it matches with a category present in the white list than it will open the link in the browser and will not ask any question in the end. If it matches with a category present in the black list than it will not open the link will pop up a message saying "Threat Detected". But if it doesn't matches any category present in both of the lists than it will open the link in the browser and will pop up a question in the end and will black list or white list that category accordingly.

In the above scenario, we have assumed that the **category classifier** is stored on the server side. But the classifier can also be stored on the user's smartphone. As I have discussed, blocking or opening of a URL is based on the category it belongs to. Therefore, by storing the classifier on the phone we won't have to send every scanned URL to the database, thus decreasing the processing steps and increasing the processing and computing speed. When a URL is scanned, the classifier present on the phone will process it and categorise it. If the category is present in the black list, then the application will block the URL there and then. Thus there is no need to send it to the database. If the category is not present in the either white or black list or is present only in the white list, then it will be sent to the database. Rest of the processing steps will be same as they were in the scenario where category classifier was stored on the server side.

5.3.2 Data Uploading

User's Personalised security list will be uploaded to the server whenever a new category is black listed or white listed by the application installed on his device. This will allow the user, in case he switches or signs in into a new device, to import his Personalised security list to his new device.

The uploading of data to the server and retrieving it back to the user's device is done in such a manner that data integrity and the confidentiality of the data will remain intact.

The long term secret key (LTSK) that was provided by the ID storage unit, at the time of sign up, to the user and to the Backup storage unit will be used to achieve confidentiality and data integrity.

Whenever a new category will be added to the user's PSL, his/her PSL will be uploaded to the Backup Storage unit. Before uploading the data or PSL the application will create a key K using LTSK and the answer provided by the user to the security question asked at the time of sign up i.e.

$$\text{Key K} = \text{LTSK \& Security answer}$$

So, before uploading the data, for the first time, to the backup storage unit, backup storage unit will have

- User's UID
- LTSK

And the user side will have

- Answer to the security question
- LTSK
- Key K, which is created by using the above two values

Now, the application will encrypt PSL or data with a key K and will output a cipher text E_K (data) and will then encrypt E_K (data) with key C where,

$$\text{Key C} = \text{Long term secret key (LTSK)}$$

The cipher text produced after the two encryption i.e.

$$\text{Final Cipher text} = (E_K (\text{data})) \, E_C$$

Will be concatenated with user's UID and the entire message i.e.

$$\text{Final message to be sent} = (E_K (\text{data})) \, E_C \, || \, UID$$

Will be sent to the backup storage unit.

The backup storage unit on receiving the message will take the UID from the message and will look for a match in its database. The database initially will only have a UID and a LTSK across that UID. Once, a UID is matched to a value stored in the storage unit, it will use the LTSK stored across that UID and will decrypt the message. The message left after the first decryption i.e. E_K (data) will be stored across the UID that was concatenated with the message.

After storing the result of first decryption, storage unit will send back an ACK and a new key (K_N) both encrypted by the LTSK to the user. I.e.

$$\text{Cipher text} = E_C (\text{ACK \& New key } (K_N))$$

It will now save the new key (K_N) alongside the present LTSK (Key C) which is stored across that UID. Next time when a user will upload or will request a backup, he will use this new key (K_N) to encrypt E_K (data) or the backup request before sending it to the storage unit. Thus, after every successful uploading or backing up cycle a new key will be generated and will be designated as K_{N1}, K_{N2} and so on. This key K_N will be used for the next communication cycle and K_{N1} for the cycle after that and so on. So, the backup storage unit will store **two** keys at a given point of time. One key will be the one which will be used in the next cycle and one that was used in the present cycle. For example, after the completion of the first uploading cycle backup storage unit will have key C i.e. LTSK and key K_N. And after the completion of second uploading cycle it will have key K_N and K_{N1}.

On receiving the new key (K_N), the application will use this key and the answer to the security question to generate a new key (K_1) which will replace the key (K). Key (K_1) will encrypt the next bunch of data to be uploaded and will send it to the storage unit. i.e.

$$\text{Cipher text} = E_K (\text{data})$$

This data will over write the previously uploaded data. In the next cycle key K_1 will be replaced by key K_2 and in the cycle after that key K_2 will be replaced by key K_3 and it will keep going on like that. All this is done in order to make sure that same key is not being used again and again. To improve the security users will also be asked to update his answer to the security question monthly or weekly.

So, after completion of one uploading cycle, backup storage unit will have

- User's UID
- LTSK and the new key K_N
- Encrypted backup i.e. E_K(data)

And the user side will have

- Answer to the security question
- New key K_N
- Key $K_{1,}$ which will be created by the above two values

And after second uploading cycle backup storage unit will be having

- User's UID
- Key K_N and key K_{N1}
- Encrypted backup i.e. E_{K1}(data)

And the user side will be having

- Answer to the security question
- Key K_{N1}

- Key K_2

And so on...

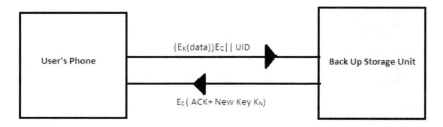

Fig. 5 Interaction between smartphone and storage unit

By communicating in this way, we are achieving **confidentiality** as data stored in the storage unit will be E_K(data) i.e. cipher text. By **Confidentiality,** sometimes called as **Secrecy,** I mean assuring user that his data was not viewed or seen by an unauthorised person i.e. any person who doesn't have an authority or required privilege to view that data, by any means, will be able to view or read that data (Martin, 2012). To view or read this data one should know key K, which is only known to the user. Thus, no one other than the user will be able to view that data.

Data integrity means once an authorised user has created, transmitted or stored a data, any unauthorised modification or addition to that data will be detected, not prevented, and the authorised user will be made aware of it (Martin, 2012). Which means this technique will also provide **data integrity** as the data is stored as a cipher text in the storage unit, thus any alteration to it will produce a new cipher text which on decryption will produce a plain text that will be different to the plain text that was encrypted in the first place. And thus, any alteration made will be easily detected by the authorised user.

5.3.3 Data Retrieval

If, for any reason, user switches to a new device then he will have to install the app on his new device. Once the installation is done, user will enter his email id and password to sign in. This information will be sent to the UID generator, which will use these two values to output a UID. As per the property 1 of UID generator, it will output a UID that will be already stored in the ID storage unit and will then automatically delete these inputs. The ID storage unit will match the UID with the UIDs stored in the unit. On finding a successful match, it will first contact the backup storage unit and will retrieve both the keys present in the backup storage unit across that UID. Both the keys and the UID will be sent to the user through different hops.

At this point of time, considering two uploading cycle has taken place, Back up storage unit will have

- User's UID
- K_N and key K_{N1}
- Encrypted backup i.e. E_{K1}(data)

And the user's app will have

- UID
- K_N and K_{N1}

Now, the application will send backup request to the backup storage unit, encrypted with the key K_{N1} sent by the ID storage unit. The storage unit will encrypt the last encrypted backup i.e. E_{K1} (data) and a new key (K_{N2}) with key (K_{N1}). Storage unit will discard LTSK and will store K_{N2} alongside K_{N1}. On receiving a reply, the app will decrypt the message using K_{N1} and will ask the user to "Enter a password", that password will be the answer to the last security question that was asked to the user before switching to the new device.

At this point, user's app will have

- User's UID
- K_N and K_{N1}
- Answer to the security question

The user app will now use this answer and key K_N to produce key K_1 and will discard key K_N. Using key K_{N1} it will first decrypt the message sent by the storage unit. After successful decryption of the message key K_{N2} will be retrieved from the message and the user's app will send an ACK to the backup storage unit that it has received the message. Key K_{N2} will be stored in the app while key K_{N1} will be discarded.

So, at this point user side will have

- User's UID
- K_{N2}
- Key K_1
- Answer to the security question

Then, finally it will use key K_1 to decrypt the encrypted backup and will retrieve the PSL.

5.4 Anonymity

Providing user anonymity is one of the model's primary aims and by anonymity I mean users identity and his/her IP address should never be revealed to the server i.e. server should only get the message from the user and should never be able to know from where and who sent that message. The first problem i.e. from where the data came from can be solved by using the concept implemented by Tor. According to (Anon., n.d.) "The user's software or client incrementally builds a circuit of encrypted connections through relays on the network. The circuit is extended one hop at a time, and each relay along the way knows only which relay gave it data and which relay it is giving data to. No individual relay ever knows the complete path that a data packet has taken. The client negotiates a separate set of encryption keys for each hop along the circuit to ensure that each hop can't trace these connections as they pass through". Thus, by implementing this technique data transportation anonymity will be achieved i.e. server will not be able to retrace the received data to his source A demonstration of which is shown in fig 2, where data transmitting from user app to the server goes through different hops. Selection of the hops will be random i.e. some messages can travel from hop1 to hop3 to hop2 to server and some may travel from hop2 to hop1 to hop3 to server.

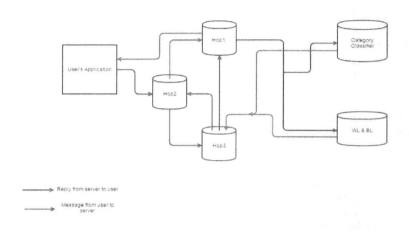

Fig.6 Anonymity model

Now that we have achieved data transportation anonymity, the second challenge we face is protecting user's id, which in our case is UID, from getting exposed to the server. But if we recall property 3 of the UID generator i.e. UID generator will work on the principal of One-Way function i.e. the function should be easy to compute and hard to reverse, (Martin, 2012). It means that UID generator should compute UID in polynomial time whereas finding the email id and password from the UID should run in exponential terms (Martin, 2012). And to eliminate any chances of retrieving the email id and password, UID generator will automatically delete user's email id and password once the UID is created, which means even if the UID generator is almost a one-way function even then UID generator's input will never be recovered from the UID. So, even if someone, with a malicious intent, at the server side becomes aware of the user's UID, that person will still not be able to narrow down that UID to any particular user. Thus, keeping user's identity anonymous and providing user absolute anonymity.

Chapter 6

Conclusion and Future Work

6.1 Conclusion

In this thesis I showed how NFC works and how the data is transmitted between an NFC tag and a smartphone. I also discussed despite being a useful and hard to hack into technology, it is still vulnerable to a lot of threats. The proposed **Security model** provides security against the discussed threat in an effective manner. The most important part of the model is the training of the different ANN's and once the training is completed and we have a database of white list and black list, we can start executing the model. The unique feature of the model of allocating users a UID and not storing their credentials provide users anonymity and allows them to check URLs anonymously. Another important component of the model is the category classifier. It classifies URL's into categories and stores these categories instead of storing each single URL in the user's personal security list. Thus, saving memory space. This, PSL allows user to create his own personalised white list and black list database.

I also discussed that a key is key shared between the backup storage unit and the application stored on the user's phone. This key not just allow users to upload and backup data but also allow user to create another key which will encrypt the data to be uploaded i.e. the data is stored as cipher text rather than in plain text. Thus, providing them data confidentiality.

All these multi-functionality of the purposed security model makes it competent in achieving thesis primary goal and simultaneously providing user added security features like confidentiality and anonymity.

6.2 Future work

The main aim of the future work will be to make the security model feasible for practical implementation at a relatively low cost.

Thus, in future I would like to design and implement the training algorithms for the neural network. It will help me to identify and solve some practical issue that might arise like providing security should not affect the overall communication speed. The algorithms will be designed for all the counter measures discussed in the thesis but I will aim to allocate them different priority level. This prioritising will help in decreasing the threat detection time (threat detection time is the time calculated from the point a URL is scanned by the smartphone to the point an output is generated on the user's screen, after being analysed by the security model) and will enhance the overall efficiency of the model. For example, while detecting an adult page, number of images on a page can be given higher priority in comparison to highlighted word. So if a URL is scanned, the ANN will first look for images and then for highlighted words. In case the output value of the images parameter is well high then the threshold value, ANN will declare it a threat without looking for highlighted words. Thus, decreasing the threat detection time and speeding up the whole process.

Bibliography

A., 2010. A symmetric Key Crytpographic Algorithm. *International Journal of Computer Applications,* Volume 1.

Abd Allah, M. M., 2011. Strengths and Weaknesses of Near Field Communication (NFC) Technology. *Global Journal of Computer Science and Technology,* 11(3).

Anon., 2015. *WebPulse Site Review Request.* [Online]
Available at: https://sitereview.bluecoat.com/sitereview.jsp

Anon., n.d. *Tor: Overview.* [Online]
Available at: https://www.torproject.org/about/overview.html.en

Attardi, G., Gullì, A. & Sebastiani, F., n.d. *Automatic Web Page Categorization by Link and Context Analysis,* s.l.: s.n.

Cassidy, R., 2007. *NFC Forum Issues Specifications For Four Tag Types.* [Online]
Available at: http://nfc-forum.org/newsroom/nfc-forum-issues-specifications-for-four-tag-types/

Choi, S., Han, S., Jeong, C.-Y. & Nam, T., August 2005. Specialized Web Robot for Objectionable Web Content Classification. *PROCEEDINGS OF WORLD ACADEMY OF SCIENCE, ENGINEERING AND TECHNOLOGY,* Volume 7.

Clercq, J. D., 2006. *Symmetric vs. Asymmetric Ciphers.* [Online]
Available at: http://windowsitpro.com/security/symmetric-vs-asymmetric-ciphers

Developers, A., n.d. *NFC Basics.* [Online]
Available at: http://developer.android.com/guide/topics/connectivity/nfc/nfc.html

Ding, X. & Pan, Y., 2006. Anomaly BasedWeb Phishing Page Detection. *Proceedings of the 22nd Annual Computer Security Applications Conference.*

Dunning, D., n.d. *Advantages & Disadvantages of Symmetrical & Asymmetrical Encryption.* [Online]
Available at: http://www.ehow.com/info_8605524_advantages-disadvantages-symmetrical-asymmetrical-encryption.html

Faulkner, C., 2015. *What is NFC? Everything you need to know.* [Online]
Available at: http://www.techradar.com/news/phone-and-communications/what-is-nfc-and-why-is-it-in-your-phone-948410

Firschein, O., Wiederhold, G. & Wang, J. Z., 1997. System for Screening Objectionable Images Using Daubechies' Wavelets and Color Histograms. *Proceedings of the 4th International Workshop on Interactive Distributed Multimedia Systems and Telecommunication Services,* pp. 20-30.

Forum, N., n.d. *What It Does.* [Online]
Available at: http://nfc-forum.org/what-is-nfc/what-it-does/

Gershenson, C., n.d. *Artificial Neural Networks for Beginners,* s.l.: s.n.

Gurney, K., 2004. *An introduction to neural networks.* s.l.:s.n.

Kay, A., 2001. *Artificial Neural Networks.* [Online]
Available at: http://www.computerworld.com/article/2591759/app-development/artificial-neural-networks.html

Kessler, G. C., 2015. *An Overview of Cryptography.* [Online]
Available at: http://www.garykessler.net/library/crypto.html

Kilas, M., 2009. *Digital Signatures on NFC Tags,* s.l.: s.n.

Le, V. L., Komisar, P., Welch, I. & Gao, X., 2011. Two-Stage Classification Model to Detect Malicious Web Pages. *International Conference on Advanced Information Networking and Applications.*

Martin, K. M., 2012. Basic Principles. In: *Everyday Cryptography.* New York: Oxford University Press Inc., p. 11.

Martin, K. M., 2012. Cryptographic Applications. In: *Everyday Cryptography.* New York: Oxford University Press Inc., p. 412.

Martin, K. M., 2012. Public-Key Cryptography. In: *Everyday Cryptography.* New York: Oxford University Press Inc., pp. 157-158.

Medvet, E., Kirda, E. & Kruegel, C., 2008. Visual-Similarity-Based Phishing Detection. *SecureComm.*

NearFieldCommunication.org, n.d. *About Near Field Communication.* [Online]
Available at: http://www.nearfieldcommunication.org/about-nfc.html

NearFieldCommunication.org, n.d. *Tag Types & Modes of Operation.* [Online]
Available at: http://www.nearfieldcommunication.org/tag-types.html

Poly, G. C., Marias, G. F. & Fotiou, N., 2012. Fighting phishing the information-centric way.

Poole, I., n.d. *NFC Tags and Tag Types.* [Online]
Available at: http://www.radio-electronics.com/info/wireless/nfc/near-field-communications-tags-types.php

Rajaram, S. et al., 2014. Vulnerability Analysis And Security System For NFC-Enabled Mobile Phones. *INTERNATIONAL JOURNAL OF SCIENTIFIC & TECHNOLOGY RESEARCH,* 3(6), pp. 207-210.

Roland, M. & Langer, J., 2010. Digital Signature Records for the NFC Data Exchange Format. *Second International Workshop on Near Field Communication,* pp. 71-76.

Sharma, V., Gusain, P. & Kumar, P., 2013. NEAR FIELD COMMUNICATION. *Conference on Advances in Communication and Control Systems,* pp. 342-345.

Stahl, A. & Ulges, A., 2011. AUTOMATIC DETECTION OF CHILD PORNOGRAPHY USING COLOR VISUAL WORDS.

Watters, P. A. & Ho, W. H., 2005. Identifying and Blocking Pornographic Content. *Proceedings of the 21st International Conference on Data Engineering.*

Zhang, H., Cai, Z.-H., Tao, R. & Li, Z.-Y., 2009. A Web Page Malicious Code Detect Approach Based on Script Execution. *Fifth International Conference on Natural Computation,* pp. 308-312.

YOUR KNOWLEDGE HAS VALUE